ARRANGE

Tom F

Duets
FOR ALL SEASONS

24 Selections for

**ADVENT, CHRISTMAS, LENT
PALM SUNDAY, EASTER
MOTHER'S DAY, FATHER'S DAY
THANKSGIVING, COMMUNION
PATRIOTIC, MISSIONS EMPHASIS**

**ACCOMPANIMENT TRAX AVAILABLE
CD & CASSETTE**

Lillenas PUBLISHING COMPANY

Kansas City, MO 64141

Topical Index

Alphabetical Index

Change words V-day

Next time

Go Light Your World

Words and Music by
CHRIS RICE
Arranged by Bruce Greer
Duet arrangement by Tom Fettke

I Will Be Christ to You

Words and Music by
MARTY PARKS
Arranged by Marty Parks
Duet arrangement by Tom Fettke

Expressive ♩ = ca. 69

Low voice solo (or unison)

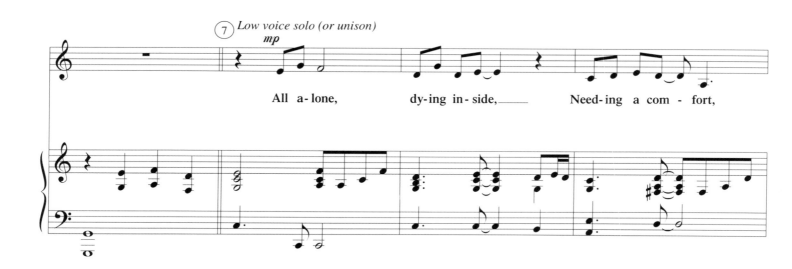

All a-lone, dy-ing in-side, Need-ing a com - fort,

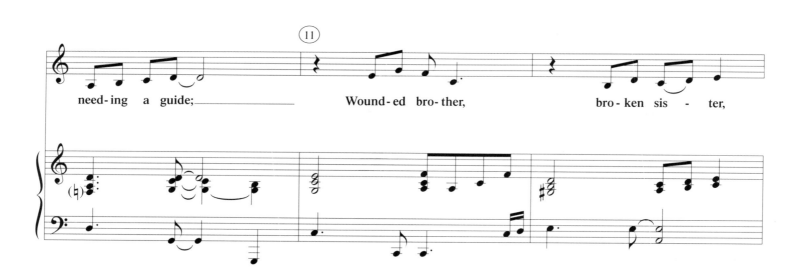

need-ing a guide; Wound-ed bro-ther, bro-ken sis - ter,

In the name of Je - sus take my hand.

16 *mf Both voices unison*

I will be Christ to you, I will be Christ to you;

C   F   G sus   G   F/G   C   F

20 *Divisi*

I'll be His hands to do what I can, Be -

G sus   G   G7   E   A m   G   G9   C

2nd time to Coda
(to pg. 15, meas. 38)

24

cause He has loved me, too— I will be Christ to

D m   F/G   G/F   E sus   E   E7   D m   F/G   G7

Let Freedom Ring

with

My Country, 'Tis of Thee

Words and Music by
NILES BOROP
and KAREN PECK
Arranged by Camp Kirkland
Duet arranagement by Tom Fettke

*"My Country, 'Tis of Thee"

Give Thanks

Words and Music by
HENRY SMITH
Arranged by Tom Fettke

We Gather Together

Netherlands Folk Hymn;
Translated by Theodore Baker

Netherlands Folk Song
Arranged by Doug Holck
Duet arrangement by Tom Fettke

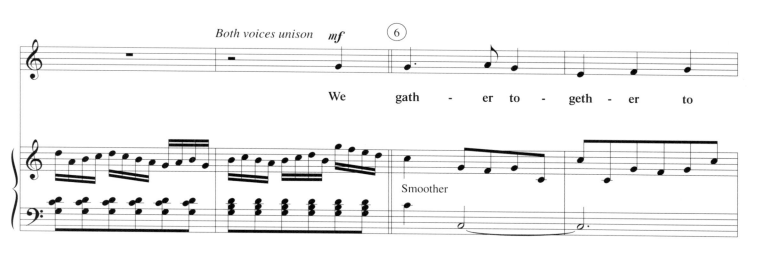

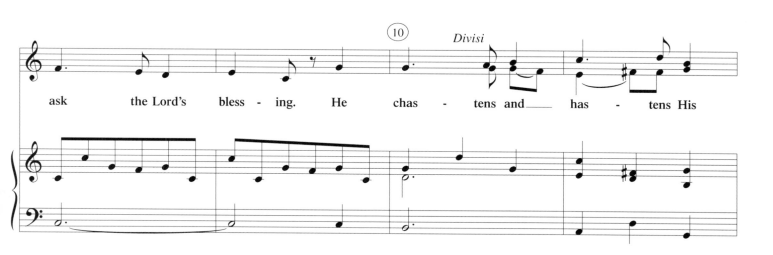

name be ev - er praised;____ O Lord, make____ us free!

A - men, A - men, A -

men, A - men, A - men, A -

men,____ A - men, A - men, A - men.

Hosanna, Loud Hosanna

JEANNETTE THRELFALL

Gesangbuch der Herzogl, 1784
Arranged by Doug Holck
Duet arrangement by Tom Fettke

Be Ye Glad

Words and Music by
MICHAEL KELLY BLANCHARD
Arranged by Bruce Greer
Duet arrangement by Tom Fettke

In these days of con-fused sit - u - a - tions,___ In these nights of a rest - less re - morse; When the heart and the soul of a na - tion___ Lay wound - ed and cold as a corpse. From the

grave of the in - no-cent A - dam_____ Comes a song bring-ing joy to the

sad; O your cry has been heard and the ran - som_____ Has been

paid up in full, be ye glad. O be ye glad, O_____ be ye

glad._____ Ev - ery debt that you ev - er had_____ Has been

Low voice solo (or unison)

Divisi

Unison

Divisi

49 *High voice*

Low voice
glad!

51 *f*

So be like lights on the rim of the

wa - ter, Giv-ing hope in a storm of the night;

Unison

Be a

55

ref - uge a-midst the slaugh-ter

Divisi

Of these fu - gi-tives in their

58 *rit.*

High voice solo (or unison)

mp

flight!

For you are

rit. *decresc.*

Behold the Man

Words and Music by
JIMMY OWENS
Arranged by Tom Fettke

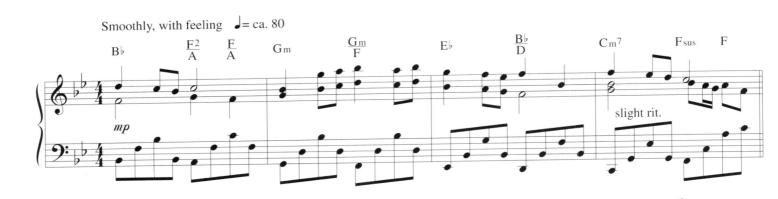

For God So Loved

Adapted from Scripture by
STUART DAUERMANN

STUART DAUERMANN
Arranged by Tom Fettke

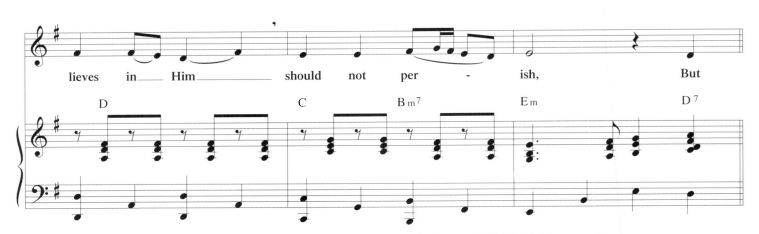

I Cannot Tell

KEN BIBLE

Traditional Irish Melody
Arranged by Camp Kirkland
Duet arrangement by Tom Fettke

Ten Thousand Angels

Words and Music by
RAY OVERHOLT
Arranged by Tom Fettke

Expressively, with a slight feeling of rubato ♩ = ca. 84

1st verse: Both voices unison
2nd verse: Solo or both voices unison

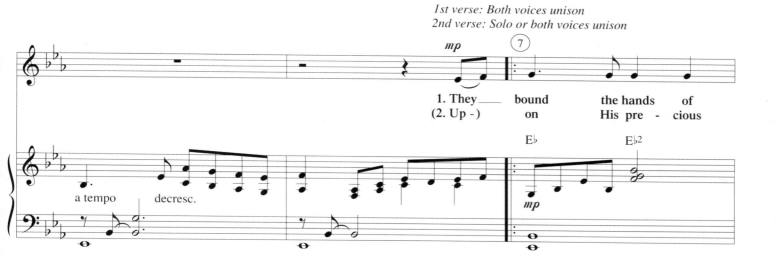

1. They___ bound the hands of
(2. Up -) on His pre - cious

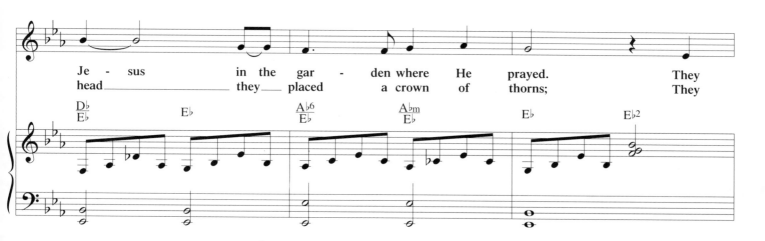

Je - sus in the gar - den where He prayed. They
head___ they___ placed a crown of thorns; They

He Is Risen Like He Said

with

I Know That My Redeemer Liveth

Words and Music by
STEVE PETERSON
Arranged by Tom Fettke

*"I Know That My Redeemer Liveth"

I know that___ my Re - deem - er liv - eth.

He is not here, He's ris - en; the gift of life is giv - en, For

He o-ver-came death's pri - son and He's ris - en from the dead.

Dry all the tears of sor - row, we have no grief to bor - row;

Now we can face to - mor - row for He's ris - en like He said.

He is not here, He's ris - en; the gift of life is giv - en, For

Lord, from Your Hand

KEN BIBLE

English Folk Melody
Arranged by Bruce Greer
Duet arrangement by Tom Fettke

ho - ly life for mine.

Divisi Now from Your

Now from Your

G 2   C M⁷   G 2   C M⁷

mf

lips_____ I hear the words: "This is My bod - y and My__

lips,___ Your___ lips I hear the words:_____ "This___ is My bod - y and My

G 2   C M⁷   G M⁷   C M⁷   G 2   C 2

blood."   I see the mer - cy in Your_ eyes,   I see the

blood."_____   I___ see the mer - cy in Your eyes,

D 7/sus   D 7   C/D   D 7   D/G   C M⁷   G 2   C M⁷

Remember the Lord

Words and Music by
DICK and MELODIE TUNNEY
Arranged by Tom Fettke

re - mem - ber the Lord.

life, re - mem - ber the Lord.

God of the a - ges, Sav - ior of man,

Might - y Re - deem - er, the great I AM, great I

Far Above Riches

KEN BIBLE
Inspired by Proverbs 31:10-31

TOM FETTKE
and *Schlesische Volksleider*, 1842
Arranged by Tom Fettke

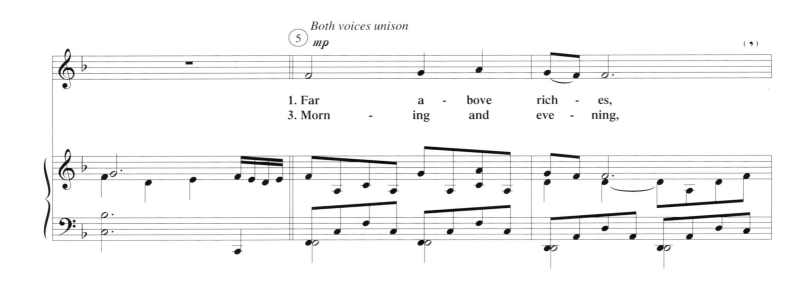

1. Far a - bove rich - es,
3. Morn - ing and eve - ning,

Far a - bove hon - or, Last - ing
Sum - mer and win - ter, Ev - er

Slower, more freely

21 *Divisi* *mf*

Mel.

2. Wo - man of hon - or, Price - less com - pan - ion,

25

Wife and____ moth - er and faith - ful friend,

29

Shep - herd and ser - vant, Teach - er and help - er, She

33

D.S. al Coda
(to pg. 88, meas. 1)

lives a love that has no end.

CODA

care.

4. God of all com - fort, Foun - tain of bless - ing, Ev - er lov - ing in all You do, Thank You for giv - ing

God of Our Fathers

with

Faith of Our Fathers

DANIEL C. ROBERTS

GEORGE W. WARREN
Arranged by O. D. Hall, Jr.
Edited for duet by Tom Fettke

*"Faith of Our Fathers"

God Is with Us

includes
Behold, a Virgin Shall Conceive
God Is with Us! Alleluia!
"Alleluias" from *Christmas Oratorio*

Arranged by Tom Fettke

*"Behold, a Virgin Shall Conceive"

12 * "God Is with Us! Alleluia"

* "Alleluias from *Christmas Oratorio*"

Baby, What You Goin' to Be?

Words and Music by
NATALIE SLEETH
Arranged by Tom Fettke

Ba - by,_____ all the world is watch - in',_____ all the world a - waits

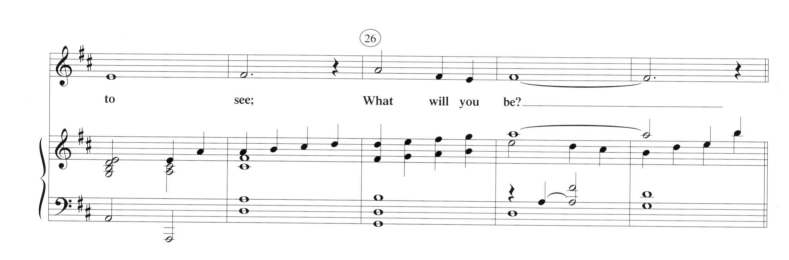

to see; What will you be?_____

Low voice
Ba - by,_____ sleep-in' in a sta - ble_____ un-der-neath the

High voice mp
Oo_____ Oo_____

heav - en,_____ What you goin' to say?_____

Oo_____

Ba - by,_____ did you bring the Good News?_____ Did you come to

Oo_____ Oo_____

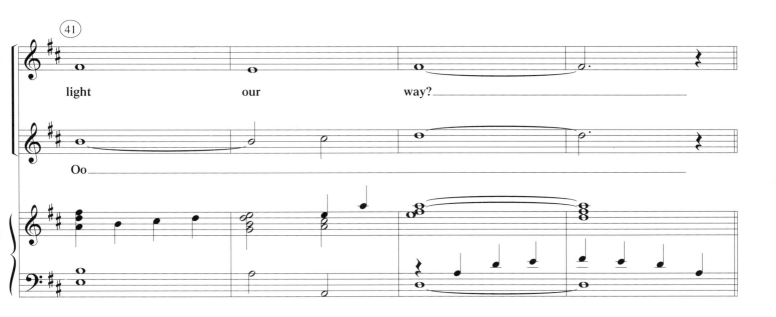

light our way?_____

Oo_____

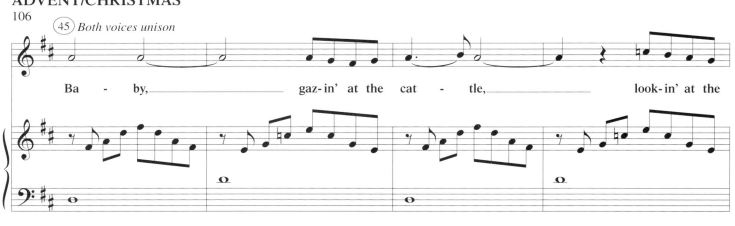

Ba - by,_____ gaz-in' at the cat - tle,_____ look-in' at the

shep - herds,_____ What you goin' to do?_____

Ba - by,_____ will you be the Mas - ter?_____ Will you bring the

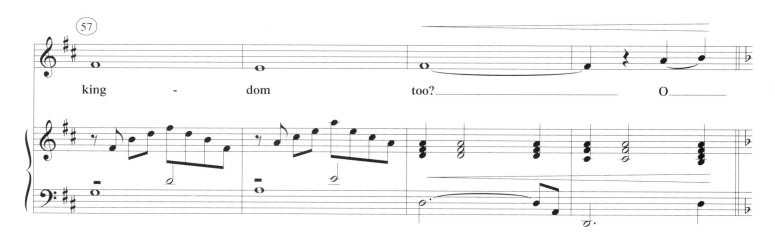

king - dom too?_____ O_____

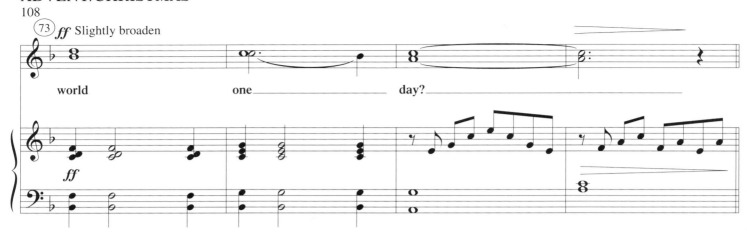

world one_____ day?_____

Slowing little by little

High voice
Ba - by,_____ ly-in' in a man - ger,_____ Will you save the

Low voice
Ti- ny lit- tle ba - by, ly-in' in a man - ger

mf Slowing little by little

world_____ one day?_____

Will you save the world one day?_____

Ped.

Sweet Little Jesus Boy

Words and Music by
ROBERT MACGIMSEY
Arranged by Bruce Greer
Duet arrangement by Tom Fettke

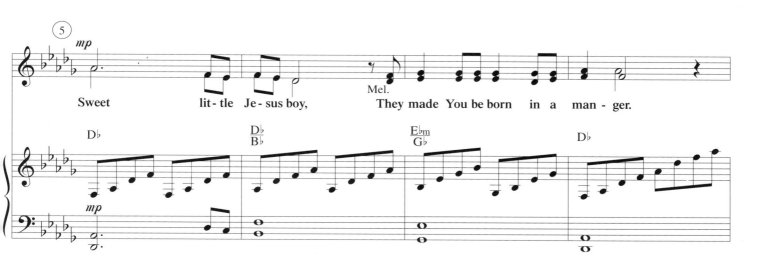

Sweet lit-tle Je-sus boy, They made You be born in a man-ger.

Sweet lit-tle ho-ly Child, Did-n't know who You was.

Rose of Bethlehem

Words and Music by
LOWELL ALEXANDER
Arranged by Richard Kingsmore
Duet arrangement by Tom Fettke

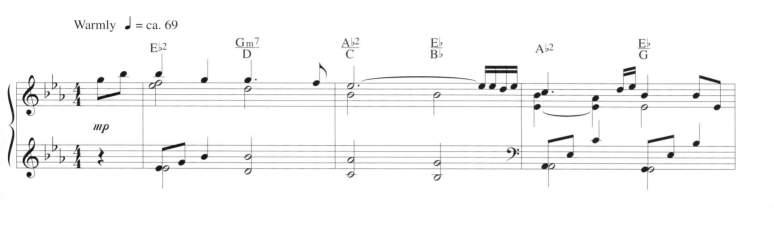

Both voices unison

There's a

Rose in Beth - le - hem, with a beau - ty quite di - vine. Per - fect

Sing We All Noel

includes

Deck the Halls
Sing We Now of Christmas
Come, Ye Lofty

Arranged by Tom Fettke

*"Deck the Halls"

1st verse: unison melody
2nd verse: parts

1. Deck the halls with boughs of hol - ly, Fa la la la la, la la la la.
2. See the Ho - ly Child be - fore us, Fa la la la la, la la la la.

'Tis the sea - son to be jol - ly, Fa la la la la, la la la la.
Rise and join the an - gel cho - rus, Fa la la la la, la la la la.

13 *Divisi both times*

Fill the world with sounds of Christ-mas, Fa la la la la la, la la la.
God is good be-yond all mea-sure! Fa la la la la la, la la la.

17

Sing, for God Him-self is with us! Fa la la la la, la la la la.
Gave us ev-er-last-ing trea-sure!

(to pg. 121, meas. 5)

21

Fa la la la la, Fa la la la la, Fa la la la la, la la la

26 A little faster ♩ = ca.100

la.

*"Sing We Now of Christmas"

Wonderful

Words and Music by
BILL and ROBIN WOLAVER
Arranged by Camp Kirkland and Tom Fettke
Duet arrangement by Tom Fettke

We Have Seen His Star

Words and Music by
BILL BATSTONE
Arranged by Doug Holck
Duet arrangement by Tom Fettke

We have seen___ His star,_____ ris-ing in___ the night._____

Fol-lowed it___ to find_____ the King___ who came_____ to bring___ the ray of light._____

Un-der-neath its beams, He was born to-night And we'll

wor-ship Him. We'll wor-ship Him. We'll

wor-ship Him this night.

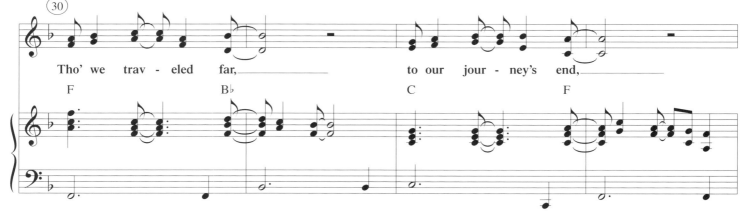

Tho' we trav-eled far, to our jour-ney's end,

Prince of Peace

Words and Music by
TWILA PARIS
Arranged by Bruce Greer
Duet arrangement by Tom Fettke

Steady, with expression ♩ = ca. 94

Low voice solo (or unison)

1. There is no hope_____ for a world that de - nies_____ You, Firm - ly be - liev - ing a
2. There is no peace_____ for a new gen - er - a - tion Liv - ing and grow - ing in

lie, Hid - ing the hearts_____ while the minds an - a - lyze_____ You;
fear. There is no home_____ in a god - less na - tion.

come and reign,
Peace, come and reign, come and reign, Set Your
G A/G F♯m D/F♯ G2 A/G
55
feet on the moun - tain - top a - gain.
D2/F♯ E/G♯ G/A
rit.
Broader ♩ = ca. 94
Take Your throne, right - ful
59
Take Your throne right - ful
B♭/C C F N.C. B♭ C/B♭
Broader
Lord.
63
Lord, right - ful Lord. Prince of Peace come and
F/A Am7 F/A B♭ C/B♭ B♭ F/A Dm C/D

reign for - ev - er - more.
Prince of
Gm7 B♭/C C Dm Gm7 4 Am7 B♭ C/B♭ B♭
67
Peace come and reign for - ev - er -
F/A Dm C/D Gm7 C/G B♭/C C
(,)
more! For - ev - er - more! For - ev - er -
71
rit.
N.C. B♭/F C N.C. B♭/F C N.C. B♭/F C Fsus/C
8va
74
ff
more!
B♭ C Dm C/E F

Lord, from Your Hand

KEN BIBLE

English Folk Melody
Arranged by Bruce Greer
Duet arrangement by Tom Fettke

Soon turns strangely thin
G/D C/D G C/G G
R.H.
24
duet
Low voice solo
mf
Come Spir-it
N.C.
Bm7 Em9 Em9
8va
L.H.
27
Come our hearts con trol our spirits long to be made
N.C.
mf
Both voices divisi
31
Unison
whole let in-ward love guide ev-'ry deed By this we
Em9
Gm/C